BETWEEN THE EARTH AND SKY

ELEANOR KEDNEY

POETRY

C&R Press
Conscious & Responsible

BETWEEN THE EARTH AND SKY

For my brother,
Peter Roy Kedney

Contents

III

IV

Harmonica

When it was clear my brother
wouldn't kick his drug addiction
and return to all the things he was great at—
baseball, tennis, downhill skiing—
he still played the harmonica.

Once, at a summer wedding, in the lull
between the toasts and dessert
he took the band's mic,
tossed his curly hair to one side,
and put the blues harp deep in his mouth—
puckered lips, blocked tongue,
the bending sound like a train
going through a tunnel.

My mother stood and clapped.
That's Peter, she kept
saying. *That's Peter.*

                    His eyes closed
to everyone in the room.
"Not Fade Away" took all his breath
to play.

I

After a Death, I Take a Walk

The cactus wren trumpets
Come here, dear, come here.
The sun rises gently,
staghorn spines soften in the light,
and the sloped back of the Catalina Mountains
slumbers in its own shadow.

The dog leads me into the wash
to a quail eaten in the night,
a boneless pile of feathers. The scent holds her.

The cactus wren's raspy, high-pitched notes
lure us back toward the house.
It's good to linger in the cool wind swells,
budded leaves, green on the desert willow,
before the day's heat declares itself, *god,*
and the ungroomed silences pass
between the living.

My Brother Pruning the Sweet Gum Tree

My brother, six feet tall and tan,
pruned the sweet gum tree he planted.
His jeans hung loose on his hips,
bare chest glistened as he sucked in death,
Marlboro Man-style, the cigarette cradled
in his lips, his ribs ready to burst
through skin as he grabbed a branch.
Burgundy-stained calluses from the resin,
stripped branches between hands
that could break a fat limb, double-sized fingers
from hard work. He released a branch
and it snapped back. He was quick, maybe high,
and shivered in the heat. His uncomfortable body
pivots in and out of shadows next to mine,
needle-scarred arms reach beyond himself.
I watch sweat and dirt drip down his face,
the curly hair tangled on the back of his neck.
His eyes look small in their sockets, fixed on me
as he grabs another branch and points
to the shoots that steal the tree's life.
He mumbles after decades of alcohol,
says it will be my job to prune the tree
when he's gone. And I never did.
His organs shut down, and the tree
comes back to life, more full, every spring.

Apple Pie

I found my father sifting,
fine white flour falling into drifts
in the belly of a yellow bowl.
He turned the crank
and metal moved like a scythe
against mesh. He was quiet,
looked young under window light,
his cheeks ruddy, his Brylcreemed dark hair,
slick and combed high,
the tip of his tongue on his lower lip
like when he wrote Christmas cards,
marking extra dots above *i*'s,
adding curlicues to the tails of *g*'s and *y*'s.
I wanted to know his thoughts.
The Cortland apples, peeled and cored
while I slept, waited on the counter
dressed in cinnamon and sugar
as if it was a special occasion, though
he often made pie early in the morning
—his pie pleased and inspired praise.
He'd serve me a piece and look into my face.
I knew I couldn't someday make pie
and it would taste like his—
the crust flaking when it hits the tongue,
the apples spicy-sweet and buttery—
but I listened to what he wanted to tell me
about measuring Crisco and chilling dough.
He had no written recipe, only his ease
cutting in shortening, his wrist moving back
and forth as if rocking a cradle.

His big fingers handled dough like delicate fabric,
easing it into a pie plate, fluting the crust
with his thumb, his mark. He set the timer
and it ticked away our minutes.
The morning of his wake, my mother threw away
the last piece of apple pie to make room
for cold cuts, salads, and sodas.
I lifted it out of the garbage and ate it.

Reading Frank O'Hara after My Mother's Death

I buy an *Arizona Daily Star* to read obituaries
in which everyone was kind, generous, and will be missed.
The heart doctor's advice:
"Don't look at the stat monitors;
you can't live by the numbers."
There were days hers were so good.
This month, a blue moon on New Year's Eve.
The housekeeper at the Waldorf, a Russian Jew, told me,
"Get out and walk. Don't look at anybody,
don't go into stores, just walk."
In St. Bartholomew's church,
a woman turned to a man—
"God wants you to live as long as possible."
I just wanted quiet.
The kind of quiet that comes out of stillness:
hummingbird wings sculling the air;
Ave Maria sung as liturgy by an opera singer.
I took a wrong turn today up the mountain.
Now, I wear blue topaz, the color of my mother's eyes,
oval stones in a bracelet, hoop earrings.
Though I am not vitreous or mineral
I have been touched, turned, warmed, and cut.
I want to believe the dog kisses my lips
because she loves me and not for the jam
in the corners of my mouth.
Now, I count lights when I drive,
snack instead of eat meals.
Now, the wave of a bare greasewood in the wind,
the orange flowers that hang on
the Cape honeysuckle in January amaze me.

The Study of Rivers

Between stones a rill where water slows, beyond
turbulence. My hatred for a brother

was a receded wave, to say it existed
would be treason—the relief I felt when he died,

perfectly normal, I'm told; he stole more
from me than watch, ring,

gold chain: a rambling laugh, a whirling dance.
The movement of sediment

complex—stream power, sheer stress,
water depth, particulate size—

a river flows toward another body
of water, sometimes never reaches one,

ends its course in the ground.

Stellar's Jay

At the edge of the evergreens,
a Stellar's jay pecks at a tree
and looks at me, tilts its black crest
toward the roots, sensing my sadness.

Like the Stellar's jay that mimics
the warbler's feast of self,
I mimic a lively voice.

Ilka, a wilderness trekker
who studies the meaning of bird calls,
said, *If you want to learn about yourself*
and how you carry energy,
walk into the forest and see
how the birds react to your body language.

I approach and it flies away.
I hear it in the distance,
lone and noisy, a thing of dusk.

How can I walk with ease
when my friend is dying?

River Waves

At Isar, water constricts over rock
and creates a standing wave.
To surf is to travel fast while not moving.
I face upstream to catch the ellipse
between a risen body and sky.
Would it be easier if my brother,
on methadone, wrote in a card, *Dear Sis,*
I was difficult to live by, or he passed the soup spoon
and talked across the table? The longest ride
on the Severn Bore is seven-point-six miles.
The flood tide surge shifts the crest against motion,
disturbed water, the depth stalled in forgiveness.

Fifty-Nine-Cent Toy

I was happy with plastic man
on a donkey with a tube
from the donkey's chest
to a rubber ball I'd pump
and air would make it gallop.

The landlady let me play on her porch,
away from the other kids on the block.

The man on the donkey was going to places
on the postcards my father sent me—
Rock of Gibraltar, Malta, Madrid.
He rode until it was dark and disappeared.

On other days, he'd appear
out of the shadows riding toward me,
a strange cold air on his cheeks.

At the Cemetery

The Christmas carnations
on my mother's headstone
laid their brown heads down.

I dust the snow off her name.
An old man, a row away,
must have heard me.
A cap in his hands, he says,
*Don't cry, she's at peace,
no rent, no cooking.*

The old elm branches
wrapped in ice hang low on the hill.
Such a cold and long white sky.

Identifying My Brother's Body

Beyond the morgue glass,
white plastic on a steel table
raised into bright light.

Only the face shows.
The mouth parted, silent lips.

I look at his closed eyelids,
his sunken cheeks,
the small birthmark on the left side of his nose.
I want to uncover his curly brown hair.

A woman is waiting for me to nod, *Yes,
it's him,* my brother, six feet long and tarped.

Nausea circles in my tight belly.
I doubt, though I'm sure it's him.

Father chokes into a white handkerchief.
The woman pulls the gray curtains shut.

Between the Earth and Sky

Though we stayed until dark, my brother died alone in the hum of
a white room.

*

The priest's boisterous laugh at the burial as I held clumped dirt in my fist.

*

Tony said my brother drank gasoline on a dive bar dare.

*

I left the Bronx hospital at night, the strangers in the parking lot.

*

A junkie at the wake scratched his arm and shook hands with Dad.

*

Methadone clinics are unmarked gray buildings between the earth and sky.

*

Outside the methadone clinic a guy tried to sell my brother heroin.

*

We pulled the plates off his broken truck and left it on the street.

*

His body, for us to name, raised on the morgue slab behind a window.

*

The tree he planted is tall and leafing and breathing and bleeds.

II

Postcards

A gull and I are the only two on the beach, feet planted
on the breakwater. The gull looks left, right, out to sea,
and occasionally at me. I think about the postcards
from Nice, Madrid, Tangiers. *Dear Darling Daughter,*
Daddy misses you, Daddy can't wait to see you.

My father would walk in with drunk sailors
after three days in port, a porcelain doll
from Greece, a baseball mitt, a valentine
for my mother.

The numb quiet would turn into squeals and claps,
the landlady bringing coffee cake and our neighbor,
Joe, piling lobsters in the sink.

Yesterday, I overheard a man on the train
say to a woman, *Sometimes it's too hard*
to receive love. I remembered my father in his dress whites.
I'd run to him, my arms a wreath around his neck,
the familiar beer fresh on his breath. I'd learned that
my father's job, as a boy, was to look out the window
and let his mother know if his own father walked straight.
His younger brother fell out of a tree and died in his arms.
He joined the Navy at seventeen.

When all the sailors were gone, he'd sit at our table
with a glass of milk, an unlit Viceroy. I'd beg my mother,
take the candy heart.

Uncles

My mother's older brothers were the beggars
I knew growing up, the knuckles on our apartment door,
their car driven onto the sidewalk, the engine left on.
Four wild fists, boiled red faces
begged my brother and me for quarters.
My mother wagged her finger like a billy club,
warned us not to give them drink money.
They sang, "Nobody likes me, everybody hates me,
I think I'll go eat worms,"
and we edged away from our dinner.
They acted like gorillas,
chased us screaming around the parlor,
nicotine and coffee-stained teeth, the roar.
My uncles sat me on their knees,
told me my father fed twelve hundred sailors
candy apples at Christmas, asked me over and over
what kind of beer my daddy drinks,
Knick er bock er beer! I'd say, making them laugh.
My mother called them *sons of bitches* and kicked them out.
I gave them the change in my pocket.

Shades

My mother was sixteen when her mother died.
The shades were drawn on the house
where her body lay in the parlor.
People came to the wake with homemade cakes
and brown liquor.

By the time I was sixteen, my mother buried
four sisters and four brothers.
When the last died, she stayed up all night
drinking beer with ice cubes,
the TV blinking in the dark living room.
The white shades marked amber by nicotine,
thin and papery as moth wings.

What We Didn't Say

It started with my mother's tongue
burning like a habanero chili pepper.
Now, her abdomen burns.
I drive her from doctor to doctor
for cultures, scopes, and scans.
Sometimes after an appointment
we stop at a deli, split an egg salad sandwich
and a chocolate chip cookie.
All we talk about is the mysterious burning.
We go over the drugs she's tried:
antidepressants, antispasmodics, narcotic analgesics,
thinking we've missed something.

Desert Spiny Lizard

Blue-green throat, black collar,
its head moved slowly in my palm
as though roused from deep slumber
and not the moment before death.
I nest it behind sage, scales flare against rock.
The next morning it's gone,
I believed, to eat ants and smaller lizards.

Later, outside my door, camouflaged in gravel,
fixed brown eyes behind pearl-gray lids.
I waited with warm hands cupped around its still body.
When my mother's eyes closed,
and I took her last breath into my throat,
I held her with nothing left to try. I buried the lizard
two inches in the ground. Next spring,
in the warm weather, it might crawl out of the earth.

Living Legacy

Imprinting hot Sonoran sand, I trespass
under barbed wire onto land
where Victorio, the Apache leader,
hid from U.S. soldiers in 1878.

*

My family is dead,
a friend called me the *legacy holder.*
I hunker in the cave's black light,
my unrest, unspat grit.
I step out of the cool grave—
the cicadas' sharp song in the dry heat,
the Dragoon Mountain peaks
break the long sky.
Driving home, wind shirrs through boulders,
echoes haunt the spaces
between them for less than a minute,
because all echoes cease.

I Woke This Morning Surprised to Be Fifty, and My Husband
Smiles at Me in Bed

My father had shore leave and we took a bus
to watch my brother pitch on a muggy June afternoon.
His fastball dazed the best batters
and Dad, too. I huddled next to him
in the bleachers, but all eyes were on my brother,
everyone yelled, *C'mon Pete.*
One, two, three, another inning in his pocket.
I tugged on Dad's shirt, bent his fingers back,
Daddy, take me for ice cream.
The purple-black raspberry, two scoops on a cake cone,
and it was just Dad and me.
The cheers grew distant,
the field's floodlights lit the sky.

It's been sixteen years since we stood in the wind-whip
on Saint Mary's hill and buried my brother.
I didn't know that I'd be unsettled,
strong-armed by old hurts, his pinning me down,
the anger, middle finger, storming from the dinner table,
my stolen jewelry, *You're ugly and no one will ever want you.*

Now, I wonder what it was like to hear
the crowd stand and clap for him,
look up and see my father's empty seat.

Memories of My Father

Dry leaves gather in the hemlock tree,
a few tuck between the fence's slats.
I rake what's scattered on the grass,
brown-edged, curled hands beg for the limb.

He'd drink and rip up money at tax time,
shredded twenties fell from his pockets
onto the dining room floor.
I'd tape them back together.
The leaves scrape across the steps,
I bag them and tie it shut
and there are always more.

Riverbank

American beech, roots tangled
in the understory, the bank scoured

by wind and rain—eroded earth, a miracle shift—
the flow still confined, broom sedge

alive, a coppery glow. Our dreams as sediment
turn into rock—last night, I heard:

Don't take Valium anymore to fall asleep.
If you continue what you are doing, you won't be here.

The dying say what they will miss the most
is their body. How long I've judged the smallest things

to be *another*. I inspect the damage,
right the canoe, paddle alongside wood ducks,

warm and dry in cold moving water.
A split branch points upward—the sky has always been there.

After a Monsoon

I lift a desert millipede on a stick,
watch it coil into a ring of armor.

I've tried to grieve my brother for twenty years.
I tried to write about running
into an old friend of his, off drugs,
a steady hand on a coffee cup. About a young man
in New York City, well-dressed
in a tweed coat, wavy brown hair,
unconscious in a pharmacy doorway,
my brother's face in his face
and I couldn't look away.

About his first day home from prison
in the shabby light of our parents' living room.
My brother, as a boy, broke every toy he touched.
The phone calls from his friends for years,
I couldn't say, *He died from an overdose.* I said,
He's pruning a tree, He's in California,
I haven't heard from him.

I put the stick in the dirt and the millipede uncurls,
vulnerable in the light, moves in a wave,
some legs never touch the ground.

Bug

The amber insect resembles a bark scorpion
with long patellae and chelae,
scurries across the Saltillo tile toward my bare feet.
I jump back, hold the eager hound's collar in my hand
and yell my husband's name. I want him
to put a cup over the stingless bug,
circling and darting between us,
slide a thin piece of cardboard under the legs,
release the dark eyes into the night.
When he walks through the door, I palm his shoulder muscles,
rest my breasts against the cradleboard
of his ribs as if the danger were real.

Love Poem

The rabbit's placid, black eye
watches me as I walk the dog
along the fence where it sits,
plump and anchored in its body,
gray fur brushed by a winter breeze.

After midnight, I bring lettuce
and watch it chew,
the calm settlement of stars.

At light's first glance, the rabbit
on its side, eyes open, ears back,
the crown of its head settled in the notch of a tree.
Its face without pain consoles me.

Rain comes and seems like old rain,
empty sky, washed dust.

A Fire Hydrant on Camino De La Amapola

We walk past it every day, it's easy
to forget its patience, reliability, fortitude.
I put my ear close to the continuous rush
of the swift underground river.
It never moves, even on muddy days,
the storm rain up to its feet.
I'd like to know stillness—
emotions roiling in the belly
while the body is calm.
It waits to be needed. The word *open*
and an arrow cast to guide the wrench's turn
if fire were to grow beyond a flame,
when we could lose everything dear, it gives,
full-on, what we are mostly made of.

Twenty-Fifth Wedding Anniversary

We walk along the black mangroves at Pelican Bay,
a baby alligator postures on its mother's head,
safe in the water, under a low-slung Florida sun.

Many afternoons, I played a wave, rode your back
because I couldn't swim. You taught me how to float
in an emergency, one hand cupped under my head,
the other, a shelf where my back rested. Then you let go.
There's nothing more you could've done, you said,
as I held my mother's urn on my lap.

We walk miles from the south to the north bay bridge,
salt-frayed air, turtles surface on the berm,
lizards rush into the saw palmettos,
our threaded hands sway under the cloud shadows,
the sky silver.

III

Ajoite in Quartz

Rough-edged, hard as knuckle.
Bottom indented like a palm,
the stria is a short, broken lifeline.
Small rock cut from larger rock,
I remember the hand of my older brother
around mine, the busy road.

It's cold at first, becomes warm in my hands,
I bring it to my lips, smell earth,
run my thumb along the yellow-brown.
His flesh stained by nicotine.
Mineral in milky quartz,
blue-green veins in muscle pink,
my brother, addicted to heroin,
yanks me back to the curb.

Turning on a Dime

4:05 a.m., a voice that sounds like me
says, *Goodbye.*
Black spaces, the sun
trying to rise in the south,
pushed east by storm clouds.

The bare palo verde bloomed when?

I'm at the doctor's and I don't want to
be there, and I walk into a door.
It's a message, it stings,
my left eye pulses.

Who coined the phrase "turn on a dime"?
My husband doesn't know either,
but points out a dime is smaller than a nickel
or a penny, and I imagine
turning myself around.

I'm Gypsy Rose Lee, throwing a boa
over my shoulder, saying,
I did it for you, Mama.

It's a long way to walk,
but a pretty Latino girl is having her Quinceañera
in Embarcadero Park—ice-blue ruffles,
black hair in an updo, a troupe of kids around her
shuffle toward the Pacific. I begin to stir
a story about young lives, beauty
not yet betrayed, but a kite is feeling
the wind tugging at its string, poor thing
caught in a tree, caught in a tree.

Checking the Stove

I try what the new therapist suggests—
feel each knob between thumb and forefinger,
the resistance, a pause and sip of breath:
off-off-off-off—in the OFF position.
I write the date and time on a pad I carry
like a mudra, repeat the numbers out loud,
and still wonder if it's off all day.

House keys, car keys, pocketbook—
I'm off and punch in the alarm code,
press the AWAY button. I am the urge
of a kettle before it cools. I stand at the stove.

The dog thumps her tail,
her affectionate stare makes me less anxious.
Off, no gas smell, no flame, no heat.
I look to her, say, *I'm leaving*,
turn the corner, punch in the code, press
AWAY.

When the garage door opens, daylight finds the walls,
the car motor revs and calms,
and I rub my palms on the steering wheel, feel the circle.
If I don't leave now, I'll be late, if I don't check,
something bad may happen.

I stare at the black knobs' white compass
needles angled at zero degrees.
The dog comes over and I break—
touch her soft ears, give a biscuit,
and smile at the way her whole body wiggles
with happiness before I check again
and head toward the door.

A Jar with a Lid

Glass unto itself is true. Formed from heat
and sand, it's solid and liquid, and neither.
A tall cylinder, etched with diamond shapes,
channels soft-blue light.
Its spun neck couples with a white plastic lid.
Sunflower butter, or seashells, or pennies in it.
Its flat bottom rests on uneven surfaces.
How can a jar seem so content?
The air inside was the wind,
the world whispers over peaks,
in seltzer, through trees, combed fields.
Some say the air is quiet for a moment.
Some, the empty jar is full.

A Park Bench in Prague

It accepts everyone who makes it there.
Cradles them in oak and iron. Bolted to the earth,
weathered, it's steady among grief,
a tantrum, mumbled conversation, *shit.*
Not different or better if we sing, kiss,
tell a joke. The bench is a sanctum,
a place to remember the dead, watch.

In the summer heat clouds flush pink,
the Charles River ripples in the light,
and a teenage girl on the footbridge models
a blue-green jacket, an ochre pencil skirt,
next fall's fashion. I forgot the ways I died,
and summon the clothes I wore,
the way my sweater and hair smelled,
the sound of his voice.

Canceled Flight

Sitting against a white oak, your arms draped over my shoulders,
        we lingered.

You said you'd cancel your flight, spend a second night—

full bloom of reprieve, first love since divorce,
        your body my cocoon.

Soon, my brother's death turned me around, blindfolded
        as in the game, blind man's bluff.

I listened for your voice before walking in any direction.

        You drove me home from the morgue.

Decades pass, we attend another funeral sermon on heavenly
reward,
        wonder which one of us will die

before the other. Talk of wishes—yours for me, mine for you
        when the body left behind is entombed in loneliness.

The conversation jumps to the good wine, crusty bread
        held like decrees in our palms,

coy smile, slight touch

    while families pulled in kites, and children squealed
        and complained,

because they wanted to stay in the park
        and couldn't
            wish the day longer.

Sunrise

My friend who is Shoshone
tells me the most important thing
is to welcome the morning sun.
Each thing in nature does.
Ground squirrels face east,
paws together for minutes.
The birds sing *to* the morning.
Even the wind breezes across the desert.
He takes his hand drum out of its bag,
and I learn gratefulness,
a tree that's been cold all night
warms in the sun when no one watches,
a young sunflower turns to the light all day.

Ripe Plums

The best plums are where branches fork,
eastbound leaves on young limbs.
I hoist myself up
toward the ripe ones on top,
shake the tree until plums fall
toward your face,
stems, leaves, the bruise
of a plum against a branch.
Your laughter blesses the earth.

We picked on a wet day,
hiked home in the mist, eighty or so
in a straw basket,
sweet, to be sure, and tart,
mud-anointed purple skins.

Loss

Fall afternoons were warm, hummingbirds feed,
my husband hadn't shorn the Cape honeysuckle's orange flames
and this morning, a freeze.
The desert willow sheds leaves.
The bare shrub won't survive.
The agate sky, more white than blue,
empty of wings.

Rio Grande

It's the silt and slope whether it meanders or braids.
Sediment from a cut bank buries a soaked hill

downstream where birds rest their wings, the gullies
cut across the floodplain. An addict is a wanderer

far from the source or confluence with another,
fluctuating between *aloneness* and *loneliness*.

Fractures and faults, the path of least resistance,
depression in the slack water in the inside of the bend.

Everywhere, depth patterns. I walk the riffle's crusted edges.
On the loop, a wishbone-shaped branch. The geese's

synchronized wingbeats: a draft of leaving.

Bumper Sticker

My brother was a John Doe overdose at a gas station,
after a month-long coma he wrote his phone number,
case closed. The report didn't mention his truck.
Sirens pass, soda cans drop into the vending machine's mouth,
and the sergeant's front desk phone rang.

Two young cops looked my father and me over
and took us in their squad car. They chatted about where
to go for dinner, ran red lights, checked their watches
and yelled, *Do you see it yet?* over their shoulders.
Our breath against the window glass.

Yards from a Getty station, "Same Shit, Different Day"
popped on the chrome bumper. A loss can be turned around.
He swaggered up to the house the day
he got the truck, talked about the money he'd make,
places he'd go.

Heap of four flat tires, dented doors, missing battery,
the saws and tools he got for his birthday gift, gone,
along with the climbing ropes to prune tall trees, clear high wires,
or rescue a cat in a storm. The front seat was covered
in a cardboard sheet, a crushed Marlboro box on the dashboard,
the empty glove compartment where he kept his wallet.

The cops said, *It's not worth towing, let the city pick it up.*
One handed my father a crowbar and they turned away.
My father pulled off the license plate. I scarred the registration sticker
with a key, stripped the tree service decal with his name,
Peter Kedney.

Old Man in a Drugstore Parking Lot

He told the threadbare joke how Van Nuys
got its name, like we were chums
who sat on a stoop and shelled peanuts,
and knew an old woman or two
who closed their curtains against the dusk.
His hand tapped my arm and hung in the air
as he tried to remember where his daughter
lived: Colorado, California, or maybe *my* town.
The sky muddled with snow,
Stonington Road with black ice,
the long drive flecked by how I dismissed his delight.
I followed the yellow truck lights home.
That night, lying alone, the windows without curtains,
sycamores leaned their elbows into the room,
the church bell marked every hour.
I slept on the floor in the new house
and thought of my father serving me apple pie,
and lifted my body, heel to the floor.

Tandem Bicycle

I ride behind my husband
along Sconset Road to the Atlantic.
He knows the path, and as he yells
downshift, I pedal slower, hoist off the seat
at *stop* and watch cars in the rotary. To *go,*
I lean over the handlebars, push off
like lovemaking, a stronger start
at the crossroad on the rise. I yell *coast*
to see the cranberry bogs, bee boxes on stilts,
an egret still as a stock photo on the pond.
At the woods' edge, berries. But, the doughnut shop
is gone. I can't bike this many miles
on my own. Sweaty and tired, we listen to the ocean
pull back waves, over and over again.

For Myself

After my mother's burial
I watched more sunsets than sunrises,
my hands startled mourning doves into the air.
Even water tasted strong.
Her nephew sent a poppy seed cake
to keep their Easter tradition alive.
Though I didn't have cancer or Alzheimer's,
I wanted to be with the terminally ill
in the hospital's qigong class, *Gathering Rice*.
Feet rooted, bow-like hands bent to the floor,
we offered the polished pearls to ourselves first,
soft mouth, belly, the sky, hands turned inward,
repeated ad infinitum.
Our open arms collected *qi* from the vault
of sun, moon, stars, through the crown
to the *dantian* below the navel, full cup.
We made a fist and cloaked it,
fingers, palms, palms over fingers,
thumbs tucked. I bowed, lifted bones,
returned to emptiness.

My Amazed Self That Sings

It knows what it is,
as if heart and brain are entrained.
Silent and solitary, strong in its stand
as the sculpted young *David*.
Air and ocean in hand.
Rhythms and beats, vowels,
crestfallen chords in the throat.
A mimic that amplifies my voice,
orca, lyrebird, echo.

IV

Famous Rivers

The Columbia tumbles twelve hundred miles, the Volga
flows into the larger Kama, Oka, Vetluga and Sura.

The Thames in London, short and mighty. The Rhine,
a fought-over script—part brook, part falls, an abundant waterway.

The Zambezi rises in ash wetland. I'd tap-dance
on the kitchen linoleum floor, step onto stairs, spread my arms

wide open, sing off-key, and imagine applause.
My dead brother's dry needles rust under the red carpet,

I promise my father I'll keep our surname alive,
rub the headstone's hard "K" onto paper, into my hands.

Most recognize the fertile Loire, the goddess Ganges,
the Nile that bends among wind-carried sand,

but not the Sepik that winds serpentine, undisturbed,
the Rio Orinoco, Steenbras, Kartong, and the Fitz Roy.

The Waimakariri, briefly known as the Courtenay, the Po
or the Ebro, unless you stand within earshot and listen.

What We Do

He tells me I will never be alone.
I hold him before he leaves the bed. He holds
my hand when we lie together and talk.
He rubs between my shoulder blades
where grief is held in my body.
I pet his head, massage his scalp
when he can't fall asleep, even if I'm tired.
If I cook eggs, I give him the unbroken yolks.
He walks the dog in the desert night,
puts the bungee cords over the garbage can.
I do the dishes when it's not my turn.
He pays the bills, balances the checkbook.
I shop for food, clean the house, launder the towels and sheets.
He doesn't understand how I listen to rocks
but lets me bring them into the house.
I bought him a menorah, lit it with him,
and learned to make matzo ball soup.
I remind him to call his father.
He loves the dog and all animals.
He lies close to me when I cry in the middle of the night.
I tell him he is handsome. I'll be there for him
when his father dies. I get up early in the morning
to make sure he takes fruit to work.
I show him the yellow caterpillar
I hold in my palm that will turn
into a Hummingbird Moth.
He believes all life is sacred.
I read him this poem.

He canceled business trips, conference calls,
and left work early when my mother was in the hospital.
I take care of him when he is well and sick.
He drives me back and forth to visit my mother
at night when I'm exhausted.
I gave him scuba diving lessons as a gift,
and I don't know how to swim.
He is patient with my OCD, puts up with my impatience
and messiness. I encourage him to sing
and tell him he has a good voice. I talk through my dreams.
He helped with the memorial, doing what I asked.
I went with him to the doctor when his retina was torn.
He skipped gym workouts to visit the hospital.
He calls every day to check on me
the way my dad did with my mom.
I make snack bags for us to take on the airplane.
He makes me laugh with silly clichés.
I check in with him if he doesn't call,
the way my mom did with my dad.
We'll take care of each other when we are old.
I root for the Patriots with him and make guacamole.
He gave me the best birthday card ever.
We lie on the floor with the dog.
We ride a bicycle built for two.
He walks on the street side of the sidewalk
to protect me from puddles and cars as his grandmother
taught him to do. He told my mom, as he did my dad,
he will always take care of me.
He would marry me again.
I only swim with *him*.

Drop Leaf Table

We bought it from a second-hand shop—
top marred, a loose hinge, scuffed legs,
oak stained honey brown and lacquered
to shine, a deep grain like old rivers
that carved their way into clay
how a path lays down under feet.
Its sides down, the plank in the middle
is a footbridge, hands cross in conversation
where we meet leafless under a new sky,
offering fresh figs to each other. Open,
it's oval, more the shape of a man-made lake
than the moon that redefines its shape,
full, crescent, waning as if to make us pine
to be different, while a lake's edge seeps
into the earth, collects and gets deeper
where it's contained, always moving from the center
of itself.

A Metal Folding Chair in the San Pedro Riverbed

Water carved away the earth, the current
laid a chair on its back, closed, amnesiac, rusted.
We imagined it was open once, its feet planted
at a picnic, a concert, a hill to watch fireworks.
The sun baked mud into cracked clay,
grasshoppers jumped on the metal frame.
The shaken trees balled into themselves.
We left it. It didn't seem like it wanted to be lifted
or cared that it was in a dry riverbed,
or that I shot a still life of it put to rest.

Eclipse over the Snake River

The twilight shimmers with an ever-driving darkness
on the surface. Diminished warmth
and light as in a sunset.

Otters slip into the water and their heartbeat slows.
Songbirds go quiet, and spiders
dismantle their webs.

After a month-long coma,
once he could breathe on his own,
my brother pressed the call button for methadone.

The nurse said, *He needed rest,*
and she drew the shades.
Midday turned into night.

Believing Is Seeing

I read in a book a Native American man made it rain.
He knelt beside an ordinary stink bug,
fat-backed and black, poked it with a stick
to make it run and turn, tapped it
until it nearly raised itself on its head.
Thunder rolled, again and again.
What was missing from the story
was how he did it, the words of his prayer,
believing in the spirit in a bug.
If only I knew there is more than what I see,
the parched desert, blue sky for miles,
and that asking for what is needed is an acceptance
of myself, then the elements, being
alone with the earth so she will speak to me.
I don't know what he said. The thirsty *cacti*
and *javelinas* are dying in the backyard.
I put my hands together, ask for a hard rain.

Self-Storage Facility

Driving home from a late shift,
I pass the mesquite tree lit up every night—
red, blue, green and orange—

at the *U Stor*. I swear
I'll climb the chain link,
pull the current or cut a wire.

Trees need darkness, an untangled breath,
to bloom, set seed, lose leaves.
My mother smoked in the dark,

my father left in the middle of the night,
and my brother died before dawn.
I know the night sky

harbors black holes,
the event horizon drags back light,
and the gravity of our ancestors.

My mother didn't want to leave,
but I whispered *It's OK*
when I tended to her body for the last time.

I, too, need the darkness
to bloom, set seed, recycle
as the hearty mesquite drops
roots
and finds water.

The dead are not our absences,
they are the luminous stars
named in our lifetime.

There are those who believe
we travel to the boundary and fall in,
but the day I brought my mother's ashes home,

I heard footsteps outside my bedroom.
The lights flickered on and off
when my cousin repeated her name on the phone.

I secure unit 643,
the number of my childhood
house on Lorraine Street.

I tell the old shaggy tree,
this is where we bring our treasures,
important papers that belonged to loved ones,

the broken cane rocker, chipped Elvis mug
from Vegas, the wobbly table
where my grandparents had dinner conversations.

I explain its crown of bright colors
lure others whose sadness is boundless—*rent here,*
this is a happy place.

Bulbs swag across its crooked limbs,
golden beans drop, feathery leaves
hide its thorns.

A Level

Air, spirits, silence
in a rectangle, a sanctuary.
Planed and weighted for the hand,
it's the way a frame begins,
a calculation ends, the center.

Plumb among walls, ceilings, floors,
the untamed landscape.
Accurate and sensitive, always ready,
the bubble behind glass
seeking the highest point.

A Long Period of Sadness

Wind pushes the edges of my house,
it curls a fan dance, murmurs
close to the ear, sweeps down my neck.
There's solace in peeled oranges, softened cheese.
The moon drops,
seeds blow in from a distance.

The wind is a dangerous thing,
knocks at the screen door.
It doesn't say, *yes*, it throats a hollow, *no*.
My palms press against the window,
feels like an echo, *no more*.

The sky tumbles and brightens.
There's solace in canned goods,
panfry, thick slices of cornbread.
Fruit drops, the calling
of my name stops—released
from what failed to bloom.

Childhood

She was a howler with a bad leg,
a dim light in her brown eyes, ears low,

followed me from room to room,
pawed the back of my calf

as if to say, *turn around.* She hid
behind my skirt when a door slammed

or a man spoke. I kept her
and thought no one would understand.

My father drank and broke furniture in the night,
returned to the Navy ship before dawn.

I held the hem of my mother's dress,
she lit a cigarette and cooked breakfast.

*

I stop a chore when Jackalyn runs
circles around the couch, pull her frenetic body

to mine and kiss her snout. She nuzzles my hand,
pushes into it when I stop petting.

When the coyotes gather in the wash
and yip, we find each other and howl,

full throttle, singing the way children sing
before they learn not to.

Deltas

When a river reaches a larger body it slows, loses power,
and sediment drops at the mouth.

Cuspate, a tooth-like shape where pebbles and sand are deposited
onto a straight shoreline.

Birds foot, formed like a claw when ocean waves are weak
and the river flow willful. It's rare—

waves are often stronger than current. Heroin withdrawal:
vomiting, insomnia, cold flashes,

yawning, diarrhea, abdominal cramps, panic attacks,
and an overwhelming shake for the drug.

After my brother's death, I had lunch with his high school friend
Jack. Clean then, with a wife and a daughter, a really good job,

he said, *There isn't a day I don't want the heroin.*

Arcuate, fan-shaped sediments, coarse and wide, so much
tides can't carry away.

Safety Pin

I find responsibility in its name,
the sharp tip springs to hold cloth,
keeps hems from the ground.
No wonder it's queen among needles.
The cochlear-shaped cover
protects the user, a point that could draw blood.
My mother sent me to pull my father from the bar,
You're the only one he'll listen to.

Tissues

One trails the other scarf-like in the air.
They move silently up to my face,
tucked under a sleeve, or shoved in a pocket.
It's a mercy to find one when I need it.
Even full, torn, blotted with lipstick, there's always a clean edge.
You'd think it's a hard lot dealt them—
snot and spit, crumpled and thrown in the trash,
but oh, to be made from a tree,
awake to its neighbor, the crown moves to let light reach its kin.
And, to become an offering one hands to another.

Sober Best

Spring. My father would buy tall tomato plants
given a head start at a nursery, picking varieties with promise:
Big Boys and Beefsteak. The first ripe and heavy fruit dropped
into his thick hands, a feast on white bread with mayonnaise.
In the early evening, he'd give tomatoes to anyone who walked by.
Listened to strangers, his sober best. After he died, neighbors said
he made time for them. I came to understand the man, home
after twenty-three years in the Navy, who moved about the kitchen
cooking roasts, simmering brown gravy, rolling dough for pies
in silence, and holding cartons filled with tomatoes
as though they were his sweet prodigies.

A Lace Stone Wall at Randall's Ordinary

Untended on abandoned land,
the wall where my husband proposed
still stands, subdued by age, an empty pasture.
The granite loosely stacked to clear rain,
ready to shift at the edge of a sheep's hoof.
Fiddleheads nestle in sunbaked rock,
moss ingots in shaded thimble-sized grooves.
Lichen weathered the gray faces blue.
The wall remains, each stone remains
among the brilliant gathered leaves,
sod and mold, soil again.

The Offering

Driving from Shoshone to Pahrump,
I hit a female quail.
I set her still body
on the side of the road.
As darkness descends on her eggs,
her mate will call for her.

Daybreak, I fill a basin on the ground
with water, and the quail gather.
Males with full topknots and red-brown crowns
scamper among the covey of twenty.
Plump, pear-shaped bodies
circle in merriment, bright sun
after their shadows.

Movement

Among rock and gravel
an angling, bare ocotillo
leafs and flowers—
red-flame tips torch the sky.

Clouds roam
and quail chitter on the gate.
Everything bidden by the sun has risen,
among staghorn spines—
fruit and flowers and seeds.

Fallow beyond spring,
I read of the night movements
of green plants folding in the dark
then opening at dawn.
I push memory's mulch aside
and listen to my breath climb
the rungs of my ribs with more
to give this world than a long cry.

I rise to daylight,
soft and shadowless.
Rocks, too, have turned over.

Home

My dog wants to catch what moves—
quail, rabbits, lizards, a squeaky football in her mouth.
She chases coyotes out of our driveway,
the wet spots of her boundaries in the yard,
while I find solace in the familiar creosote,
the steady rock mountain views.
She taught me to claim space and join a pack.
Lying beside her on the carpet,
for the first time I let myself love a place.
I pet her brown and white fur as she rolls
onto her back, exposing her soft belly.

The View

Peaches ripen on the tree outside.
Silver-blue clouds dim the late morning glow.
A two-year-old cat sits in a window and watches
cardinals flit in the hedgerow. She's just eaten
and licked her paws clean. At three o'clock
a woman who answered the ad will come
and take the cat the girl can no longer keep.
Silence roves the small apartment. Two
bananas in a bowl have darkened and grown soft.
Their sweetness plumes the air. Both the girl and cat
are sleepy now. What strikes me is the way
the cat nuzzles the girl's thumb, and the girl sings
a lullaby over the cat's purrs. I'll pause
for them—the girl stroking the cat's black ears,
the trust it shows, rolling onto its back.
    The rain begins, droplets faint on the glass.
Streaks like claw marks blur the torn leaves,
fallen peaches on the wet ground.
A moment passes. Then the next. The rain stops
and birds collect in high branches and break into song.

Acknowledgments

My sincere thanks to the editors of the following publications in which these poems, some in earlier versions, have appeared:

American Poets & Poetry: "My Brother Pruning the Sweet Gum Tree"
Connecticut River Review: "Apple Pie"
Fjords Review: "A Park Bench in Prague"
Lalitamba: "Believing Is Seeing"
Manzano Mountain Review: "Deltas"
Miramar Poetry Journal: "After a Death, I Take a Walk"
Mojave River Review: "Childhood" and "Home"
Mslexia: "Stellar's Jay"
Mudfish: "Between the Earth and Sky"
New Ohio Review: "Harmonica" and "Postcards"
Panoply: "A Lace Stone Wall at Randall's Ordinary"
riverSedge: "Fifty-Nine-Cent Toy" and "Checking the Stove"
San Pedro River Review: "A Metal Folding Chair in the San Pedro Riverbed"
Skidrow Penthouse: "Movement"
Snapdragon: A Journal of Art and Healing: "Sunrise"
SunStruck Magazine: "Living Legacy"
The Cumberland River Review: "Reading Frank O'Hara after My Mother's Death" and "Drop Leaf Table"
The Fourth River: "River Waves," "Rio Grande," and "Famous Rivers"
The Maynard: "A Fire Hydrant on Camino De La Amapola"
The Poeming Pigeon: Love Poems: "Ripe Plums"
Turtle Island Quarterly: "A Jar with a Lid"
Under a Warm Green Linden: "The Study of Rivers" and "Riverbank"
Weaving the Terrain: 100-Word Southwest Poems: "Bug"
Write to Meow: 2015: "The View"

"Apple Pie" is anthologized in *The Writers Studio at 30*. "Reading Frank O'Hara after My Mother's Death" is anthologized in *The Cumberland River Review: The First Five Years*.
"Sunrise" was reprinted in *A Life in Service: Stories & Teachings from Mala Spotted Eagle* by Hermine Schuring.

Some of the poems, sometimes in different versions, and with different titles, also appeared in *The Offering*, a chapbook published by Liquid Light Press (2016).

In Gratitude

I am grateful to family, friends, and fellow writers and poets whose support throughout the years has sustained and inspired me. Thank you to The Writers Studio for the gift of community and a strong foundation in craft.

I wish to express my deep gratitude to Philip Schultz and Juliet Patterson for their insights on earlier versions of this work. Their advice and encouragement provided strength to persevere through difficult material.

I am especially grateful to Markiah Friedman and Mariamne Engle Friedman, who published some of these poems in my chapbook *The Offering*. They put my words into the world, and it's wonderful to be a part of the Liquid Light Press family of poets.

Thank you to John Gosslee and Andrew Sullivan for caring about this book. A special thank you to John for his keen-eye edits and resounding "You got this" when I was deepening the work.

I am grateful to my cousin Barbara Berardino for always showing up at my readings. Thank you for listening.

I offer "Stellar's Jay," "Sunrise," and "Believing Is Seeing" in memory of Mala Spotted Eagle Pope.

I am forever grateful to my father, Roy, and my mother, Helen, for believing in me. They were proud of my accomplishments, and I hold them and the memories of their love and support in my heart.

As always, I am most grateful to my husband, Peter Schaffer, whose unwavering love, friendship, and support has carried me through my darkest times. "What We Do" is for him.

To my brother, Peter: thank you for being my brother. You taught me to survive. In writing these poems, I learned that love and understanding leads to forgiveness.

About the Author

Eleanor Kedney is the author of the chapbook *The Offering* (Liquid Light Press, 2016). Her work has appeared in *Miramar Poetry Journal, New Ohio Review, The Fourth River, Sliver of Stone,* and other journals. She has contributed to several anthologies, including *The Cumberland River Review: The First Five Years* (Trevecca Nazarene University, 2018) and *The Writers Studio at 30* (Epiphany Editions, 2017). Her poem "Bubbles Blown through a Wand" won the 2019 riverSedge Poetry Prize (University of Texas Rio Grande Valley). Kedney is the founder of the Tucson branch of the New York-based Writers Studio, and served as the director for ten years. She lives in Connecticut and Arizona with her husband, Peter Schaffer, their dog, Fred, and their cat, Ivy. Learn more at eleanorkedney.com.

C&R PRESS TITLES

NONFICTION

Women in the Literary Landscape by Doris Weatherford, et al
Credo: An Anthology of Manifestos & Sourcebook for Creative Writing
by Rita Banerjee and Diana Norma Szokolyai

FICTION

Last Tower to Heaven by Jacob Paul
No Good, Very Bad Asian by Lelund Cheuk
A History of the Cat by Anis Shivani
Surrendering Appomattox by Jacob M. Appel
Made by Mary by Laura Catherine Brown
Ivy vs. Dogg by Brian Leung
While You Were Gone by Sybil Baker
Cloud Diary by Steve Mitchell
Spectrum by Martin Ott
That Man in Our Lives by Xu Xi

SHORT FICTION

Fathers of Cambodian Time-Travel Science and other stories
by Bradley Bazzle
Notes From the Mother Tongue by An Tran
The Protester Has Been Released by Janet Sarbanes

ESSAY AND CREATIVE NONFICTION

Selling the Farm by Debra Di Blasi
the internet is for real by Chris Campanioni
Immigration Essays by Sybil Baker
Je suis l'autre: Essays and Interrogations
by Kristina Marie Darling
Death of Art by Chris Campanioni

POETRY

The Rented Altar by Lauren Berry
Between the Earth and Sky by Eleanor Kedney
What Need Have We for Such as We by Amanda Auerbach
A Family Is a House by Dustin Pearson
The Miracles by Amy Lemmon
Banjo's Inside Coyote by Kelli Allen
Objects in Motion by Jonathan Katz
My Stunt Double by Travis Denton
Lessons in Camoflauge by Martin Ott
Millennial Roost by Dustin Pearson
Dark Horse by Kristina Marie Darling
All My Heroes are Broke by Ariel Francisco
Holdfast by Christian Anton Gerard
Ex Domestica by E.G. Cunningham
Like Lesser Gods by Bruce McEver
Notes from the Negro Side of the Moon by Earl Braggs
Imagine Not Drowning by Kelli Allen
Free Boat: Collected Lies and Love Poems by John Reed
Les Fauves by Barbara Crooker
Tall as You are Tall Between Them by Annie Christain
The Couple Who Fell to Earth by Michelle Bitting
Notes to the Beloved by Michelle Bitting

CPSIA information can be obtained
at www.ICGtesting.com
Printed in the USA
LVHW092154020320
648805LV00002B/507

9 781949 540093